Fragile Prisms

a Potpourri of Poetry

by

Dorothy A. Smith

PRESS

Fragile Prisms
by Dorothy A. Smith

Printed in the United States of America

ISBN-13: 978-1-60034-661-3
ISBN-10: 1-60034-661-8

www.xulonpress.com

Peace of Christ's Love!
Dorothy A. Smith

Dedication

I dedicate Fragile Prisms to my children, Annie, Billy, Paul, Jolly, and Jeff. They are my finest natural resource, providing a well-spring of ideas, support, suggestions, and stimulus; enough to last a life time.

Acknowledgements

Many thanks;

- to Erin Cunningham, my granddaughter, and valuable assistant whose computer skills are laudable. She typed, edited, shaped, and downloaded the entire manuscript with ease and confidence. Kudos!
- to my family and friends for their positive encouraging words through the years;
- to the people at Xulon Press, especially Renee Aebli, Acquisitions Manager, who made the submission process a breeze. They treated me like an old friend;
- to the wonderful people who wrote their professional endorsements, Dr. William Coulson, Mary Jane O'Brien, Lance Hurley and David Turner.

Preface

The poems in this small book are not those of a profound, ever to be noteworthy poet. They are simple and such that anyone, even you, disciplined to writing and having a sharp awareness of life and human feelings, could have written.

Writing poetry is a gift for bountiful expression that you dabble with and enjoy as a dabbler. It is an avenue of freedom with many street signs. For years I have traveled that avenue with a propensity of observing my little world and the influence of God in it. It's no wonder then that my poetry has a spiritual leaning. Poetry has provided me the opportunity to acknowledge the presence of God and convey it to my readers in poetic form.

May you find yourself smiling and musing as you read each poem. May you enjoy poetry and also give it a "go", someday.

Dorothy A. Smith

Table of Contents

Chapter Three – FAMILY AND FRIENDS.......39

Chapter Four – PARABLES AND PRAYERS 65

HEART TO HEART

Fragile Prisms

We love the quiet waters,
lapping at the shore,
the never-ending waves,
the wonder of the tides;
We love the light of dawn,
the peace of dusk,
the beauty of a star-lit sky,
and the mysteries there displayed.

We love each season of the year,
repeatedly returning,
expected,
with order and staying power;
We love growth and experiences,
learning and sharing,
and we accept life's hurtings
with blind faith.

We are grateful.
We still find awe in simple things,
like smiles and embraces,
courageous words of hope and cheer;
We love to celebrate family,
friends and neighbors,
and hold each one as a fragile prism
of light and life.

continued

We love each other even more
because through the years
we have stood side-by-side
in the midst of a powerful creation;
We have become acutely aware,
we reverence the pulse of life
from the God of the Universe
the God of Love, the God of Mercy.

We Love...

Conversion

I've known of You all the days and years
of my transparent life, and
took your benevolence for granted,
barely acknowledging Your
Son's tender passion. I even turned from
You to dote on my
own strengths which I now know
were but weaknesses.

What I envisioned as my happiest
moment became short-lived and
shallow. But always You were there
allowing me to make all
the choices that left me empty and
groping for more of the
same illusions. You knew I belonged
to You, I didn't.

Then the Paraclete in disguise entered
my life to rescue
me from the grip of despair,
from fear and trembling, from
falling from all grace; to delude the devil
and light the path
that brought me to my knees before
the blessed Sacrament;
to say as Thomas said, "My Lord and
my God", You did
not forsake me and I was not
worthy of Your love.

Yes, I have known of You all the days
and years of my transparent
life, but now I feel new life within
that challenges me to change
daily; to turn from the worldly routines
that dominate the hours of
these days that You have given me.
I have chosen to attach myself
to You, to Your will. To love You with
my whole heart, with my
whole soul, with my whole strength
and my neighbor as myself.
I have chosen to be Your servant, Lord;
to love You, to praise
You, to adore You, to thank You,
and to beg for Your Mercy.

Today is for Memories

Today is for memories
just like yesterday,
and all the days gone by.
The eyes look inward
with ranges of sentiment,
to retrieve, in a twinkling,
images which fill
the gallery of the mind.

Just like yesterday,
and all the days gone by,
sounds wind through
our secret labyrinth,
pulsating the strings of the heart
causing us
to fell again the joy
of stored up memories.

Just like yesterday,
and all the days gone by,
today, we strive once more
to do the etchings,
to record the priceless moments
that hinge yesterday
to today for tomorrow.
Today is for memories.

Come To Adoration

Come and kneel devout in prayer,
Surely, surely God is there.
His Presence permeates the air,
His graces flow from Holy prayer.

Oh, light of life, Most Holy glow,
Treasure of the ages show,
Loving You will help us grow
With the gifts You do bestow.

Grow in ardent peaceful rest
Where heart and soul unite in quest
In time suspended, triple blessed,
As the Lord's invited guest.

Blessed by Him, Creator, King
By the Spirit's strength we sing,
By the Son's redemption bring
New life from Whom all blessings spring.

Do come without duration
With neither shame nor explanation,
In His Presence give adoration
In precious, heartfelt conversation.

Life

There was a time,
just once, in youth,
when time stood still
and cares were
light and few;
when tomorrow never came
because today
was for forever.
But nothing is forever,
and time is
neatly measured
passing in a wink,
a breath,
leaving a trail
of yearnings
that linger like a fog,
then changes.
The seasons
of our life
occur but once.
Like tumbleweed
they hurry off
to who knows where,
carried by the whim of God,
by time, the breath of life.

continued

Each season is an enigma,
a mystery onto itself,
with questions
left unanswered
like why?
and dreams are
full of blemishes
that cannot
be erased
only altered
by time.
Thus life,
like time,
is neatly measured
in winks, in breaths,
in seasons,
and nothing is forever,
but once, just once, in youth,
time stood still.

If Only For A Moment

Love is like a gentle breeze,
whispering wisps that touch the cheeks,
fresh and holding pleasing, promise,
if only for a moment.
in mystic waves it moves
unpleasant feelings aside,
casts doubts to dust,
and dwells on dreams,
if only for a moment.

This gentle breeze
carries the breath of God
and touches only those who
pause long enough to grasp the gift;
who permit the fragrance
to stir the heart and lift
the soul to dwell on dreams,
if only for a moment.

Love too brings grief.
When this gentle breeze
ceases to blow, remains still,
and stored beyond reality's reach,
it looses the original hail of hope,
and the heavy heart is
crowded with dreary doubts,
and weighty wonderings,
if only for a moment.

continued

But Love, this gentle breeze,
is neither lost nor wasted
in grief or hardships, but is
made strong through tested tempering,
and the breath of God returns.
Yes, it blows fresh and light
with the fathomless fragrances
of everlasting Love,
if only for a moment.

Diamond Thoughts

Tears
can bathe
and wash away
any pent up feelings
of hurt, pain and anguish,
and bless anyone who
yields to laughter
uncontrolled in
tears.

Children,
our legacy
are heirs of
our hopes and dreams
for a better life than ours,
are bound to stumble
because we did
just being
children.

Love
is unselfish,
willing to give
all and more for
the sake of your happiness,
and seeks for nothing
in return but
to be
loved.

The
pain I
feel today resembles
that of someone in
the grapple of mourning, still
coping, intense with grief,
soundless sobs that
take too
long.

Joy
is the
gift that God
alone can give and
when delivered it rushes to
change our mixed emotions,
and fills emptiness
with pure
delight.

Dawn
reminds me
that the Lord
has granted yet another
day to live and serve;
to count my blessings;
to regard myself
grateful and
humble.

Home
is more
than structure with
windows, walls, fixtures, floors,
doors, fences, flowers, and space;
it is a sanctuary,
a safe harbor,
possession, protection,
belonging.

Springtime
peeks out,
makes our senses
teeter with blitheness as
we respond to things unseen
during the dormant winter,
and we reach out
with nature's
Springtime.

From Greeting to Adieu

'Twas the year of completions and
four years had flown
You were titled a teacher with a class of your own
And all you had memorized, learned to the letter,
Was stored with your notes,
for you had to do better;
Now YOU were the teacher and
this was YOUR school;
Get there early, stay there late,
was the unwritten rule.
Your class was a big one, not full... over-flowing.
In no time at all, all your greenness was showing.
When all of a sudden you had some misgiving,
Should you really have this job for a living?
So off to the veteran in the room 'cross the hall,
You hurried for help, for surely she knew it all,
But what in your wondering eyes should appear,
As you fumbled and babbled, a tiny-tell tear;
"Hang in there", said the veteran, oh so consoling,
"You just need a lesson in eye controlling."
With a little more practice,
and a much stronger will,
You learned in short-order that your look could kill.

More grateful than grateful,
your gratefulness rolled,
As you strove to master this new discipline mold:
Now, Stop 'em! Now, Stare 'em!
Now Glare 'em! And Dare 'em!
On Reading! On Writing! On Learning!

Don't Scare 'em!
From the front of the class! To the back by the wall!
"Now listen up! Listen up! You're mine,
one and all!"
as the rings on the water where
a pebble has dropped,
Flow out widely and calmly, the rowdiness stopped;
So on with the lessons, and on with your chore
As the veteran had taught you,
you knew you'd learn more.

And then in twinkling, it seemed a short while
The children were needing a new teaching style.
Don't rough 'em, or tough 'em,
or chide 'em, or burn 'em,
Use a Fuzzy, warm Fuzzy, that aught to learn 'em,
Soon the compliments flowed and
the Smiling Face grew,
Like a Kilroy, its image was launched
then with you;
So you put on new glasses and
your old velvet glove,
For you had a new knack…
teaching children with love.
The class was your oyster in the palm of your hand!
And the children the pearls for a most
priceless strand!

continued

31

At one time every parent was older than you,
As the years turned to years, this was no longer true;
The veteran was gone and you stood in her stead,
And shared all the tricks that were
a stored in your head;
But what's this they're saying,
that the pendulum swings?
Does this mean its time to return to old things?
To the rod? And the Rule? And perhaps eye control?
No more Fuzzies? No more Smiling?
No more cajole?
A somber look back at the rich years gone by,
Back to the Basics! Basics! Now comes the cry.
You've been through the mill,
and taken your beating.
You've grown to the Max. Who feels like repeating?
So laying your future wide open for change,
And giving deep thought, your life re-arrange;
You bow now from the books,
the objectives and goals,
The subjects you served, and institution controls.
You are freer than ever, and wealthier too,
For teaching has wrought fulfillment for you!

Adieu!

ANGELS

Oh, Angel of Mine

Oh, Angel of mine, mine alone,
how faithful you stand in my life.
You halter my pace,
least I fall from His Grace,
and you lighten my burdens and strife.

Oh, Angel of mine, mine alone,
I wish I could picture your face.
You hover above,
and you bathe me in love,
as you're guarding me from place to place.

Oh, Angel of mine, mine alone,
when my days are completed with love,
my arms open wide.
On your wings let me ride,
to that place that's prepared high above.

Angels Watching Over Me

I called out to the angels
whose choirs number nine.
I needed the protection
of their virtues so sublime.
For Satan was about me
in beautiful disguise.
He tainted and twisted thoughts
to suit his own demise.
But the Seraphim and Cherubim
and the heralding choir of Thrones,
surrounded and shielded me
to ward off Satan's stones.
Dominions, Powers and Virtues
crowded round from wing to wing.
I felt the victory in resistance,
and my heart began to sing.

Angel Talk

My angel whispered and I felt the motion.
It was deep inside, a warm emotion.
I waited for another word,
the likes of which cannot be heard.

It is an essence, very real,
the likes of which you only feel.
It is freedom, a willing choice,
to hear the words without a voice.

I see my angel though its form is spirit.
I hear my angel, in my heart, I hear it.
When my angel whispers I feel the motion,
a stirring, deep and warm emotion.

There is wisdom in the whisper sent,
and I can't explain what my angel meant.
But this I know, for sure today,
I understand in a different way.

Hello My Angel

Hello, dear Angel of mine,
you are here with God's permission.
To guard me and to guide me
is your Heavenly commission.

But there are times I need much more
to make it to tomorrow.
Like, I need more courage, and strength,
less pain, less sorrow.

I need to feel your closeness when
there is no one else in sight.
I need the company of your strong presence
to fight the daily fight.

Please forgive me when I'm thoughtless,
and I neglect to talk,
And when I forget to thank you each day
we do our walk.

Forgive me too each night when I forget to pray.
I know you love me dearly; God would
have it no other way.

So, Good morning, and Good night,
and thanks a million, hear my prayer.
Even though I cannot see you, in my heart I know
you're always there.

Amen.

FAMILY AND FRIENDS

Grannie Didn't Tell

Dear Grannie was quite special
in ways of rare intent
for she had a way of speaking,
you felt the message sent.

Often times I waited trembling
a reprimand from Dad,
but Grannie didn't tell or nod
that I'd been good or bad.

She would look at me with calmness
until our eyes were meeting,
and then without a single swat
I took a silent beating.

Nobody knew but she and I
the pain of just confessing,
and nobody felt but she and I
the healing in caressing.

For Grannie silence was golden
a cloistered treasured cell,
and trust the priceless bounty won
when Grannie didn't tell.

There was love in Grannie's lessons
and without me even knowing,
she taught me through forgiving,
poured strength into my growing.

continued

41

When all the world stands judging,
and I know myself full well,
I'll have a graceful courage
because Grannie didn't tell.

Mommy's Hands

Mommy's hands were magic,
or something great like that.
She kneaded dough, whipped meringue,
made potato-cake with a pat.

She could sew and darn and knit two pearl,
And with blithe fingers make straight hair curl.

Remove a sliver with a single jerk,
Take a broken toy and make it work.

When a light switch failed, or the water'd over-run,
Mommy's hands made fixin' fun.

She could stretch a meal, and trim the fat,
Feed us all and then the cat.

She counted pennies when we had trouble
Then with her magic could make them double.

We had great fortune, there was nothing tragic.
Through all our lives Mommy's hands were magic.

Now she folds them oft in graceful rest,
Her chores completed, she was the best.

You see her purple veins and gnarled fingers,
But something different, awesome lingers.

continued

43

For when you hold her hand she gives a soft pat,
And there's magic there,
or something great like that.

Sister Dear

Before another year goes by,
before another sun sets,
There's something I must share with you,
before my mind forgets.
I'm speaking now right from the heart
of sentimental stuff.
You'll understand these feelings though
the poetry seems rough.

Long ago God smiled on us and
He made us sister souls.
He gave us qualities that blend,
and He called home "The Molds".
You loved me then with my bouncy curls,
and even now with thinning hair;
I loved you with the bangs I cut,
though then it seemed unfair.

I marveled how you would excel in sports
and in Home Ec.
You worked so hard and did so much
while I gazed at Anton Peck.
You'd roll your sleeves and tackle jobs
with efficient ease.
While I was content to read and write
with no one else to please.

continued

You seemed to have the greatest knack
of knowing what to do.
And I, like limp spaghetti,
changed my mind a time or two.
I found in you such fortitude,
such love and open sharing.
I hope you found in me an equal love and caring.

I ask myself, "How can it be, I'm so like you,
and you're so like me?"
Some parts of us we can't define,
I wish for yours, you wish for mine.
Sure, God in all His wisdom took traits
from Mom and Dad,
And evenly distributed some qualities they had.

Then He blessed them in a special way
with daughters ever strong,
And matched us to His Image for He never
has been wrong.
Now, if He had to try again to create you,
Sister Dear,
You'd be the full embodiment of the Sister I revere.

So many times I'd like to say three
little words, that's all.
No sooner do I think of them when tears
begin to fall.
So I'll write them, and you'll read them,
because it's easier to do.
And we'll both cry, and we'll both say,
"Sister Dear, I LOVE YOU!"

Brother Dear

You often find it difficult to accept a compliment.
You shrug your shoulder and think lightly
of such sentiment.

I've always had to wonder why this side
of you seemed gruff.
Perhaps deep down, you don't resent
the words you call just fluff.

Perhaps that air of authority assumed
when you were young
Developed your autonomy of boss
on the climbing wrung.

But I have long discovered that
your disposition is a disguise
To protect the core that is you; loving, caring,
generous, and wise.

It's okay to wear that armor,
for it does command respect.
I love you, Brother, in spite of it,
and I'm sure you don't object.

Hands

These are the hands I held quite tight,
Warm with fever through many a night.
Chubby and soft, disciplined oft,
Cleansed of dirt, kissed when hurt.

These are the hands I grasp with poise
to convey achievement with my boys.
They are confident and unique,
so anchored I find it difficult to speak.

They hold me now in a different way,
protecting, worrying, as they may.
we need each other from day to day.
but theirs are the hands that hold the sway.

These are the hands, strong and grand,
Grasping my shoulder, helping me stand.
Gentle and sure, calloused and tan,
Hands of my boy, my son,
The Man.

Affable Daughter

You have a generous,
giving nature that radiates joy each day,
and a knack for solutions, you always find a way.

You have a natural sense of humor,
a very pleasant wit,
and a confidence, when tested,
bespeaks of a true grit.

You appear resilient in a protective, tortoise shell,
to hide your injured feelings you
camouflage quite well.

But underneath that strength and
edge of female power
you are as fragile and precious as petals on a flower.

The sense of pride I feel for you
gives my heart a glow
you have given me more strength
than you can ever know.

Though you are rare and so uncommon,
it's obvious to see
why I know you well and love you,
for you belong to me.

Please, Mom and Dad

Don't scold me when I'm in error,
when I've done wrong and paled.
I sense your disappointment
that I've stumbled,
that I've failed.

Don't scold me or reproach me
when I know my own misgiving,
inside I feel the pain,
your pain with mine.
I beg forgiving.

Rather hold me in your heart,
please try,
when your arms resist embrace.
Please, look into my eyes
beyond my conjured face.

Then see, and hear,
and feel my living
the torment of suspense,
just waiting
for your forgiving.

The New Chapter

You were my baby, my first,
and we bonded at the moment I
heard your first cry.

I spent hours just holding you,
and staring at every flex you made.
I was in awe.

The mystery of birth became
the mystery of life, growth and development.
I was overwhelmed.

I used Dr. Spock's book more than
the cook book. My questions were answered
on why and what to do, but a mystery remained.

Time was spent wondering, worrying,
and wishing because you were the first.
What would you be like full grown?

Well, there was something that occurred
outside "The Book". You progressed
beyond the questions and answered.

You had a determination and drive
so I released you to nourish
the dreams you harbored.

continued

51

You reinvented yourself as one
who'd take on new challenges
to succeed at creativity and life.

And in doing so, you over came
the nitty-gritty that breeds on
giving up and failure.

Thus, you wrote the new chapter in
"The Book", "How to succeed
when the pages are blank."

The Attributes of Grandparents

If I could advertise on billboards high and wide,
The attributes of Grandparents would
light the sky with pride.

My Grampa's wealth I'd mention,
he always shares his money;
His worldly knowledge I'd attest
for his stories wise and funny;
His knack of fixing things I'd cheer
he's a "Jack-of-trades", for sure,
And his strength would shine
with the confidence that heroes do endure.

If I could advertise on billboards high and wide,
The attributes of Grandparents would
light the sky with pride.

My Gramma's love I'd capture
with strokes of baby pinks,
and her eyes would beam,
like candle flicks, of steady patient blinks;
My Gramma's cures I'd surely list
for hurts and growing pain.
With hues of blues I'd print these words,
"Your prayers are not in vain."

If I could advertise on billboards high and wide,
The attributes of Grandparents would
light the sky with pride.

I Think You Know

You love me when I cease to try;
when I'm hurt and choose to cry;
when I've done well and gained a lot;
when I've worked hard and when I've not.

You love me when I've made a mess.
No matter what I do, I guess.
You make me feel like I'm a prize,
like I'm the apple of your eyes.

Well, I've got feelings much the same.
I get them when I call your name.
When I call out, "Gramma, Grampa, look at me,
I love you this much," and my arms spread free.

Even more than this, in a special way,
more than deeds can do, more than words can say.
I love you more as I grow and grow,
and when I smile, I think you know!

My Heroes

Grammas and Grampas are heroes
because they've been around a spell.
They've been there, done that and so
they prove it with stories they tell.

They know how things were and are now,
and how most things should be instead.
They have solutions to problems galore
that somehow they've solved in their head.

Like when I'm confused or troubled,
when no one can figure me out,
Gramma has perfect examples
of others the world had to doubt.

When nobody else cares to listen,
and there just is not enough space,
Grampa stops the world; helps me off,
with stories from some other place.

Someday, when my growing is through,
and when I've learned all there is to livin',
I'll be a grandparent, "I hope",
and return all the love I've been given.

Grandparents Are Very Special

I never met my grandparents
for they lived across the sea,
but I truly got to know them
and they were quite fond of me.

When Gramma heard I was born
she crocheted a little hat,
and sent it with her love
in every stitch and tat.

When Grampa saw my picture
he saw his own reflection.
My eyes were his,
likewise my whole complexion.

I heard so many stories
about my grandparents dear.
Sometimes I felt
that they were really here.

I never got to touch them,
to give a hug or kiss.
Why I feel a part of them,
I can explain like this:

I think the answer's Love,
created from the start.
The kind of Love you cherish,
snuggled in the heart.

All that I have learned of them,
and they have learned of me,
keeps us close, so close,
it's like there is no sea.

Grandparents are very special,
and no one can deny,
with Love so unconditional,
there is an eternal tie.

Crystallizing

Looking back, years back, is like
eaves dropping with consent;
like seeing through long lens binoculars;
hearing through a vacuum;
and opening sealed vessels.

It seems so natural, so innocent,
and at times quite fitting;
like reaching without touching;
believing yet wondering
about old visions blurred with sentiment.

There are tears, both choked and real,
they are warm and healing;
soaked with memories of past treasures
of youth and that longing to be free.
Crystallizing takes accounting in the heart.

And you are there, all my loved ones,
my family, my friends,
forever crystallizing into a permanent form
of value and beauty unrivaled,
of priceless crystal visions.

Dear Friend

Dear Friend,
I shall always remember
how you listened and took
my concerns to heart.

How you balanced common sense
and practicality,
and set trivia apart.

You possess the substance,
of the things that matter
in our daily life.

You maintain dignity
in your decision making
and adjust the strife.

And through the years
of grooming friendship,
of weaving lasting bands,

You've fortified me
with your strength,
sustained me in your hands.

You are unaware
of your influence
and the good that you have done.

continued

Just know that of my friends
You are a very
Special One!

Servants, You and I

We were sent, you and I,
to arrive at the same place, at the
same time, for the same reason,
to work together, to serve,
the beckon of the Master.

We did not, do not,
and will not ever see or know the plan,
but the details are revealed as
we cooperate and serve,
without a probing question.

We were chosen in spite of our flaws
and weaknesses because
our love for the Master needed tempering,
and molding, and
submission to be made perfect,
as the Master is perfect.

We are not to question the plan
when we encounter the heat of
the tempering, the contort of the molding
or the pain of the
yoke of submission because we are His servants.

We never really lose our flaws or weaknesses,
like a limp they
identify us, but are diminished as we
accept the Master's Plan,
for our sinew grows and inside we are robed anew.

It does not matter who or what disturbs
our labor today because
we are resolved to bow in humble, patient,
submission to each
beckon of the Master.

Yes, we were sent, you and I,
and God gives us whatever we need
to work His plan, to guide us home,
and to lead as many as
we possibly can to the Banquet.

A Toast To A Friend

Each one of us in passing through.
Our pathways luckily crossed.
It is the same for me and you,
We've gained more than we've lost.

How grand it is that on the way
Our company we've shared.
We've laughed, we've cried, and had our say,
And we have always cared.

You've shown your generosity,
Your open heart and more,
Your child-like curiosity,
Your diligence to chore.

You've given more than you've received,
And we are here for showing
That friends in whom you have believed
Have hearts and faces glowing.

When counting all your blessings, Dear,
On happy days and sad,
Recall the gathering of us here,
And in your heart feel glad!

For God is good and giving ever,
His blessings brightly shine
In friends of true endeavor
Like yours, and ours, and mine!

PARABLES AND PRAYERS

The Faithful and the Worthless Servant

Be faithful. Be prudent. Be Wise
while the Master is away.
Tend to your household and chores,
and never idly go astray.
Depend upon the promises,
for the Master's word is real.
Never loose heart or wane in waiting
for His reward holds much appeal.

But if you drop your guard,
and lean to lust and sin,
because the opportunity is there,
the Master, who knows all, sees all,
will return unannounced without a flair.
He will strip you, and heave you with the losers;
will yield the punishment for failing;
will send you into the darkness
with teeth grinding and great wailing.

Read   Matthew 24:45-51

At The Well

He found me at the well.
He said, "I thirst."
So I dipped into my well.
For He promised so much more
than the drop that I was giving,
my cup for His never-thirsting giving.

Though I was considered inferior,
Unfit to even speak,
He knew my whole interior,
And made me strong
Where I was weak.

Since then we daily meet
His well and mine to fill.
I need so much
and He so little
to satisfy His will.

I pray you ask me daily, Lord,
to quench your loving thirst.
And I in turn resolve
to always serve you first.

Read John 4:4-15

The Seed and The Weed

The good seed is from the Son of Man
scattered in the world's vast sod,
and the seed, the children of Heaven,
who live by the word of God.

Now, the weeds are from the evil one
seeking to choke all and deplete.
Their numbers multiply,
and defy defeat.

The harvest is the end of the age,
and the angels, as harvesters then,
will gather all evil-doers, the weeds,
and cast them into the fire for sin.

But the faithful, the children of love,
will shine brightly, as the sun.
Rewarded in the Kingdom of God,
praising forever, "Thy will be done."

Read Matthew 13: 36-43

The Vineyard and The Tender

The vineyards fill the valleys
as far as the eye can see,
and the rows are straight and strong kept
so by the Tender, He.

He tends and ties the branches where
they spring forth from the vine.
He cuts and prunes the bad growth,
and keeps the branches fine.

Then comes the harvest time,
the time He's waited for,
when all the Vineyard's vines
are loaded with fruit galore.

The call goes out far and wide for laborers each day.
All those who come to labor agree
to the Tender's pay.

And whether you labor a lifetime,
in the Vineyard of the Lord,
or just the eleventh hour,
you receive His just reward.

Matthew 20:1-16

The Barren Fig Tree

The Master of the orchard
sought fruit from the fig tree.
Three years He sought in vain.

"Cut it down", He said,
"for it exhausts the soil".
There was no sign of gain.

The gardener begged
for one more year
with promise to cultivate.

Perhaps more caring
would bring desired fruit
or the Master WILL eliminate.

Read Luke 13:6-9

Another Simon of Cyrene

Let me be another Simon.
Call me from the crowd today.
Let me help another victim
who is struggling on his way.

Let me share the burden,
and complain if it is right.
Let me be another Simon,
but this time, let me fight.

Lord, empower this new Simon
with your mercy and your grace,
to never fear the angry throng,
or a revengeful face.

I'll always stand-by ready,
Your Divine Will my desire.
Let me be another Simon,
filled with the Spirit and His Fire.

Read Luke 23:26 and Mark 15:21

God's Gift

Silence.
It is the avenue
Where grace and peace flow.

It opens the eyes,
The ears, the mind,
And the heart.

It envelops the person
And finds the soul
In silence.

It allows God
To enter, to dwell
In the silence.

Where His voice
Is felt
And peace ensues.

Prayer

Prayer is the universal language
for communicating with God.
It is read, spoken, recited,
sung and felt from the heart.
Anytime is time for a talk with God.

Private prayer is too beautiful,
too personal, to repeat or share.
It is full of awe, silent tears, and
a sentiment of familiarity with God.

We wait in dormancy for God's voice,
until He moves our hearts.
Then we are transported, enlightened,
filled with trust and a renewed hope.

As children we discover this language.
We feel inadequate, yet special because
we sense God's love, His acceptance,
and we feel encouraged to draw closer in prayer.

Now, throughout each day when we converse,
He hears and understands our human nature,
and knows we love Him even when
it is difficult to accept His will.

When we finally do accept, veiled in tears,
His words reach the shattered hearts,
"I am with you always…" and He sends
a comforting peace.

Then we make our very own prayer;
choice words; personal; surpassing all words.
These words never touch the lips,
but flow from our hearts to the heart of God.

Our Jesus

Our Jesus fell...
the first time...
the second time...
the third time...
and the flagellation was but more.

The crowd's abuse of complacency,
of jeers and scoffs
added weight and sore.

And this cross,
this humiliating cross,
He carried it.
It was for you and me
that He carried it.

He came for this,
to bare it all;
every scourge,
every fall.

To die and rise
was a surprise.
His obedience, His promise,
proved no compromise.

Listen In The Silence

Listen in the silence
ignore the noise
that crowds the mind
and drains the energy for peace.

The noise is but a decoy,
disregard it so you can
create new thoughts
of lambent light.

Create bright thoughts that lift
the soul beyond the silence,
giving impetus
to new vision and enlightenment.

Thoughts that infuse wisdom
into being alive,
that unite the beauty of just being
with the goodness of God.

For it is in the silence
that the voice of God
whispers to each heart
the reassurance of His Love.

Spirit of Carmel

I am a Carmelite
through reception and profession.
A tertiary member
and I follow in procession;
the priests, the monks,
the brothers in formation;
all the sisters and the cloisters
who pray in jubilation.

I hold as my own model,
example radiant bright,
my Blessed Mother Mary
who reigns at heaven's height.
Ave, Ave, and Hail,
O' Star of ages sung
guard my total being
my mind, my heart, my tongue.

Let every thought and breath
and even every motion,
originate from thee
with heavenly scented potion.
May I fulfill my promise
to pray and also serve,
That you and your Son
may smile on me,
your servant in reserve.

Simple Prayers

Lord,
Hear me when my voice is locked inside my heart.
Hear me when I am hurting, confused and groping.
Keep me from the darkness,
from the dingy cloak of doubt,
From the arms of fear, the clutch of failure.
Hear me! Help me! Hold me together.
Amen.

Heavenly Father,
Only you can read our hearts!
Only you can fill our needs!
Grant each one of us the strength
we need to Love and Serve you!
Amen.

Heavenly Father,
Please grant me the strength
I need to carry out the duties
of this day with Love, Patience,
Humility, Obedience, and Trust.
Amen.

continued

Lord,
Thanks for always knowing what to say,
and saying it;
for always knowing what to do, and doing it;
for always being strong,
and giving me strength.
Amen.

LIVING AND EXTINCT

What's Its Name?

When it landed on me,
I thought it a bee.
I could shake it away
but Mom said, "Let it stay."

Then she said, with a hug,
"Just be calm like the bug.
Look closely, you'll see
it's not a bee."

Red spotted with black
all over its back.
It crawled up my arm,
and did me no harm.

It seemed just so tame.
I asked, "What's its name?"
Then Mom said, with a hug,
"It's Lady Bird, Lady Beetle,
or just Lady Bug."

Chewing Their Cud

Consider the Artiodactyla,
the even toed animal order,
they graze without aid of a porter.

The deer, the cow, and the goat,
eat grass like the sheep and the antelope.

Even their relative clans
manage life without any bans.

Thus the camel and lofty giraffe find fodder
and never call out for a cotter.

With teeth like the tool called the spud
they just chew and re-chew,
and re-chew their cud.

Frail Little Lizard

creepy, creepy,
creeping through the green,
rolling, shifty eyes,
hoping not to be seen.

slowly, slowly
moving under and over,
quickly, quickly dashing
when there's a shadow on the clover.

a frail little lizard
turning brown and green,
a frail little lizard
afraid to be seen.

Purring Lions

A lion and a lioness went strolling down the lane.
He admired her tawny fur,
and she his full combed mane.
Said the lion to the lioness,
"Why do your eyes shine so?"
Said the lioness to the lion, "'
Tis you beside me makes them glow."

"I'm just a lion like all the rest,"
said he and swished his tail.
"Oh, no, you're prouder and braver,"
the lioness did wail.
So they strolled and strolled until
at last the sun lit up the moon.
And the jungle stood listening to
the lions' purring tune.

And the jungle stood listening to
the lions' purring tune.

The Terrible Lizards

Once upon a time,
I can't explain just when,
but it was long ago,
before the time of men.

Terrible lizards were here,
their fossils tell just where.
They were so frightful large,
yet traveled everywhere.

Some ate leaves and trees,
their necks were very long.
Some ate other animals,
they were quite large and strong.

Some dragged their tails
and clashing thunder made.
Some dug the earth with horns,
as if they had a spade.

They appeared quite powerful
though not so very clever.
One may have thought
they could almost live forever.

But the Ice Age came,
and turned the earth to glacial frost.
Terrible lizards, dinosaurs,
were then forever lost.

Penguin Patter

This aquatic bird sounds quite absurd
loving cold and ice, day and night.
With web-like feet, flat and neat,
and flipper-like wings, for no flight.

This penguin cute, in a classy suit
pays neither rent nor taxes
as a sub zero hero
on the tip of the earth's south axis.

Now, this old Great Auk used to be the talk
with its razor-like bill distinct,
just sixteen inches tall, not tall at all,
today has become extinct.

Poor Dodo Bird

Oh, Dodo bird, oh Dodo bird,
extinct with little fame.
The Portuguese who found you
gave you that silly name.

Your life was oh so simple
on the Island of Maritius.
Of the images there are of you,
as a bird, you looked ridiculous.

Poor bird, without a chance,
with skimpy wings and weight,
Island visitors and their animals
ate you raw and on a plate.

Now memories are but a chuckle.
Your name invokes torpidity,
and is often attached to people
who exhibit their stupidity.

CHRISTMAS GREETINGS

The Wisemen

The Wisemen came and carried gifts
as they followed bright, yonder star.
The angels sang and their voices rang
over the hills and far.
The shepherds heard the angelic word,
they sought the place of light
where Jesus lay on a bed of hay
on that, oh, blessed night.

The Wisemen and the shepherds there
all bent in awesome praise.
The angels' song lingered long.
It echoed through the days.
Of peace, oh, precious peace they sang,
God's message to fulfill,
to the trusting and God fearing,
to all men of good will.

Come from the hills and fields afar.
Find where the rich and lowly are
adoring The One True King.
Where angels sing and their voices ring;
where you'll kneel and you'll feel
the message they bring.
Glad tidings to you, and to you, and to you.
May His peace in your heart forever ring true.

Holy Happiness

When the choir sings "O Holy Night",
and "Angels We Have Heard On High";
When the spirit of the season's bright,
and the scent of holly nigh;
Remember me as I remember you,
and may your heart feel light.
For once again the old is new
with Holy Happiness in sight.

When snowflakes dance on the evergreen,
and the wind blows snow in mounds;
When the silver moon to all is seen,
and nature's beauty thus abounds;
May you feel the peace and joy as I,
to trust in His sure might.
For once again the old is new
with Holy Happiness in sight.

Yes, Holy Happiness is here,
arriving on time year after year;
recalling, reminding, reciting;
the spirit of Love still inviting;
close ranks, give thanks and rejoice;
sing out or just whisper, your choice.
For the old is made new
with Holy Happiness for you.

Herald Tidings

Herald tidings from angels,
praises of joy,
on that Holy Night,
for that Baby Boy.
Godly spirits, pure light,
still rally and sing.
In melodious lyrics
this message they bring,
"Receive Him, who is Love,
His gifts, His decree,
of bountiful blessings
for you and for me".

Revel in the joys of Christmas!

It's Time Again

It's time again
to dust the boxes
filled with garlands and wreaths,
tinsel and glitter;
to hang the lights and ornaments;
to add the potpourri of woodlands and fir.

It's time again
to come together and light the candles
of the Advent Wreath and Menorah;
to pray the prayers
of expectation and hope;
to draw the family ever closer.

It's time again
to ponder and wonder
how quickly the days have gone;
to reflect on what we've gained
in our reservoir of strength
of faith and love in caring for each other.

It's time again
to reach out not just to touch
but hold and make an imprint
on your heart with my wish
that God's Choicest Blessings
visit and stay within your home forever.

Greetings

It matters not what I got,
what it is, what it is not;
whether debit, cash or charge,
whether very small or large.

For this is what I think…
this gift is but a link.
It is weighed in grams of gold.
It is the "Thought" that ne'er grows old.

It is just for you, this gift from me.
It says I did remember.
A simpler gift there could not be,
and it is sealed in Christmas ember.

This gift, this "Thought", this link,
ties our past to "now" with cheer.
So Merry Christmas, "Special One,"
and of course, A Happy New Year!

My Wish

If I could make a wish
for a gift beneath your tree,
I'd think of you and yours
I'd have a wishing spree.
Cost would be no issue,
just delivery on demand.
It would be the largest package
all wrapped and tied and grand.
I'd have no trouble choosing
the wish to stand the test.
I'd wish God's Choicest Blessings
for you are worth the Best.

I'd sign a pretty tag
with a special guarantee,
that if my wish was pleasing,
you could send it back to me.
I would receive delivery,
to place beneath my tree,
our shared and heartfelt wish
all wrapped from you to me.
And oh, the joy of wishing
in this great Season Blest,
God's Choicest Blessings would be ours
for we are worth the Best.

From Yesterday to Today

From yesterday to today
and through all our tomorrows,
you are special to me.

Like a gift that I wished for
getting dusty with age;

Like a book that I treasure
though it's missing a page;

Like a prayer that is said
with the calm of a sage;
you are that special to me!

May the Peace of Christ's Love
touch your life!

Peace of Love

I make a wish for each New Year,
and everyday therein;
that you will find true Peace of Love
and renewed faith begin;

That your heart will feel unburdened,
and your spirit set to win
the victory of another year,
and the challenges within;

That good health and wealth
will fill your bin,
so full that trouble
dare not enter in.

May His Peace of Love
in you begin,
God speed my wish
for you again.

Ma's Gift

Ma encouraged us to dream because it was free,
and more pleasant than brooding
on what could not be.

Especially each Christmas we kids could expand
on visions of grandeur even dream out-of-hand.

She took us looking to feed all our yearning,
pointed out bargains and sales for our learning.

Then, tell it to Santa was part of the game
because in the end it was him we could blame.

With all of his rushing he did not fill our list,
and the fact of the matter, our list he had missed.

But we each got a gift though not of our greed.
Ma said it was Santa who decided our need.

She said Christmas was Jesus, God's gift to us.
On HIS birthday, HE doesn't seek worldly stuff.

So Ma let us dream with our feet on the ground.
She led us to embrace the freedom we found;

To give the self gift, a deep measured surprise;
To walk through our dreams without
closing our eyes;

continued

To love, wish and hope; to even reach for the sky;
To be grateful to God for the things you can't buy;

To give Jesus praise and always center-most space,
not just at Christmas, but everyday, everyplace.

Memories

When Christmas time is drawing near,
I wonder back alone;
To find again the memories imprinted as in stone;
To a time when we had less than
anyone else as poor;
When we had a gifted spirit, innocent and pure.

One time, the longest day we lived,
for sure, was Christmas Eve.
We waited for a Christmas tree,
as only kids believe.
We knew that tree was coming,
and we waited down the street.
When Daddy turned the corner,
he dragged one at his feet.

We helped him bounce it up the steps
and squeeze it through the door.
No stand to hold it up, so he nailed it to the floor.
Then the top part needed tending where the
branches reached too far.
He trimmed them off and held me high to hang a
paper star.

continued

"That's the grandest tree you'll ever see,
" Daddy boasted to us all.
And we agreed, "Now, that's for sure,
that tree will never fall!"
Then we started tossing tinsel and trimmed
with childish glee,
No toys or gifts that year, but Daddy got our
Christmas Tree.